"I have spe⌐
as cultivati⌐
let me just s⌐ ⌐ ⌐ ⌐ ⌐
budding Jesus movement called The Table Network.
They are a Jesus-centered, culturally vigorous,
missionally adventurous, discipleship-oriented,
church planting movement. I am excited about what
they are doing, but even more so the way they are
doing it. I expect something of the unfolding of the
future of the Christian movement in their common
work. "*

Alan Hirsch
Author of The Forgotten Ways,
The Permanent Revolution, and 5Q
Founder of Forge Mission Training Networks,
100Movements, and 5QCollective

*"The Table Network is an exciting missional
movement focused on gospel saturation in cities in
America and around the world. They are pioneering
new methods to stir up kingdom movements of
multiplication for the glory of God. Check 'em out!"*

Daniel Im
Director of Church Multiplication
NewChurches.com/Lifeway

*"The Table Network has put language to how God
has been attempting to move my thinking on
discipleship and mission for years. These people
have captured the essence of organic missional
kingdom ministry without the legalistic add-ons. "*

Mike Jarrell
Missional Catalyst/Consultant, The Creo Network
EFCA

"Being part of The Table Network has fundamentally changed the way our family views church. Through our group, we continue to discover that "church" requires both more and less than we had ever imagined - more intentionality, more vulnerability and more sacrifice - and less ritual, formula and polish. The result has been more intimate relationship with Christ and our neighbors than we've ever experienced before."

Jenna Guidi
Stay at home mother of two, Boston, MA

"The Table Network is doing the hard work of (re)focusing on the simplicity of good food, the Good News and good conversation as the central focus of God's family life. A focus with profound implications for the neighborhoods they dwell in and the leaders they are developing. The families I know and love in this movement embody the words, works and ways of Jesus. A place at your table is a place at the Table of Grace."

Caesar Kalinowski
Church planter/author of the best-selling Gospel Primer, Transformed and Bigger Gospel
One of the founding leaders of Soma Communities

"Being a bi-vocational leader in NYC allows me the opportunity to daily meet people where they are. With the friendships formed, the insights gained, and The Table Network walking with me as I go... I am seeing the good news spread and a new church family forming out of the marketplace."

Eddie Everette
Accounts Manager at Apple Inc.
& Church Planter/Pastor, Brooklyn, NY

"God, through the Spirit, seems to be refocusing the church on the worldwide co-mission Jesus left us: to make disciples. The Table Network is one of the more promising networks that are equipping leaders and churches to live into movement. Their emphasis on people finding freedom in Christ as they connect with God's new family at the table, attests to their understanding of the grassroots work of movement, for it is simple, sticky and scalable. May God increase their tribe."

JR Woodward
National Director, V3 Church Planting Movement

"The Table Network is a beautiful movement that is making stories everyday of people like me by answering the search for life's deepest desire - a authentic life with Jesus soaked in freedom and love. In their unapologetic thrust towards this end they have found their greatest impact by simply pointing to the Spirit of God that was already in the people of God in a loving and encouraging way. Simply put, they are doing exactly what God has freed us all to do, which is rare today and therefore very precious."

Jon Kapel
Boiler Operator & Planter/Pastor of The Table
Cleveland, OH

"For years I searched for a tribe focused on introducing those who are disinterested in the Church to the freedom and family found in the person of Jesus. In TTN, I have found that tribe."

Josh Chevalier
College Pastor, Midtown Church
Austin, TX

"We set out to grow food and share it at a table placed in the field on our farm. The vision was to see people gather, find rest, and to be reminded of the good things spoken in Psalm 104. At first our plans were vague until we met The Table Network and discovered an uncomplicated and powerful framework for how we would build our mission. Now in our third year, we have sat over 5,000 people around our 100 foot table and have formed a community that meets daily, dirtying their hands on the farm, sharing stories, and finding rest in the freedom found in Jesus."

Chris & Rachel Jones
Locavore Farm, Grant Park, IL

"God's Kingdom is coming and His will is being done on earth as it is in heaven. The Table Network is helping networks like mine think deeply about how we are going to reach the 70% of the population who isn't going to come to a religious service. They are enriching the conversation of how we make disciples who make disciples."

Dr. Wes Hughes
Portland Church Planting
& Urban Church Planting Catalyst NWBC

"Making disciples from the harvest for the harvest, a true lost-to-disciple-making culture, is what The Table Network is all about. In an era where there is lots of noise around the subject, crowded with many aspirational leaders and theoretical philosophers, they are actually equipping the everyday Jesus follower to be fruitful and multiply."

Todd Milby
Executive Director, Catapult/catapult.group

"As a pastor of a church planted ten years ago, I find the increasing pull to prepare for a come and see approach to gospel ministry. With a desire to make disciples in the scattered nature of our church and a partnership with The Table Network, we are seeing men and women truly equipped to disciple others where they live, work, and play."

David Hamstra
Lead Pastor at Crosspoint Church
Crown Point, IN

"Not only has The Table Network equipped me in how to live as a missionary and disciple those who are uninterested the church, they have helped me navigate through some of the religious ideologies I had developed as a pastor, a move to the marketplace, and the formation of a new ministry that is meeting my tribe where they are."

Ramon Martinez
Founder of Pure Movement &
Bay Breaks Entertainment, Tampa, FL

"The process of making disciples to see a Church form from the ground up takes a family of regular people who invest, pray, equip, support, challenge and encourage. The Table Network has intentionally positioned themselves to do that well and to see that vision multiplied. I have found strength as God worked thru the humble accessibility these men provide just about every week. As a result, Common House continues to bear good fruit."

Dan Hartmann
Telecommunications Technician &
Pastor/Planter of Common House, Grass Valley,CA

"North America is an ever-increasing salad bowl of cultures. There is no one-size-fits-all approach to Christian mission in such a diversity of landscapes. The Table Network is a breath of fresh air, integrating a flexible, bi-vocational posture, faithful to the Scriptures, committed to their neighbors, contextual in mission. They take seriously what Jesus said to do... going into their world to make disciples who make disciples, and the Father is using this powerful tribe of leaders and churches."

Travis Vaughn
Co-City Director of Made to Flourish, Atlanta, GA
Catalyst & Founding Board Member for the
Atlanta Church Planting Alliance
President of the Terminus Collective

"I have found that the business of church (i.e., budgets, buildings, programs, professionals) often distracts us from the kingdom work of discipleship. The Table Network in my view is a modern day image of the church in the book of Acts and the face of the church for the future."

Emmett Todd
UPS Driver

"Nothing is more central to the identity of a Christ-follower than their honoring God through making reproducing disciples who worship and obey Him. The Table Network is among those God is using in amazing ways to equip churches and church members to do just that. I'm thrilled to see their footprint of strategic influence expanding."

Dr. George G. Robinson
Associate Professor of Missions & Evangelism
Headrick Chair of World Missions

"When I talk to people about church planting networks or a tribe to belong to, I often tell them that the most missional network I know of, and have myself experienced, is The Table Network. They have taken years of experience in the trenches and are now helping folks apply the way of Jesus in their particular contexts. And the biggest win? They've done so in a way that is both simple and deep."

Sam Smith
Church Planter/Pastor at Reunion, Seattle, WA
Founder of Folklore

"The families I know in The Table Network "get it": the Good News of Jesus doesn't just belong in the pulpit and the pews! Like the early church, this network understands discipleship happens in relationships throughout all areas of life! I have experienced, while working with Table Network leaders, the love these families have for Jesus, their desire to share Him with all people, and their commitment to empower others to do the same!"

Paul Eller
Retail Store Manager

"The Table Network is doing a great job of leading people into life-changing relationships with Christ and then encouraging those individuals to help others follow that same path. Our team at World Partners has been impressed by their approach to the point that we've asked them to consider placing people in Europe to work and minister alongside our staff."

Dave Mann
Director, World Partners

"Being a homemaker is often a struggle that causes one to question their value, worth, and how they can make disciples in between changing diapers, cooking, and cleaning. The Table Network is intentionally helping everyday people, including stay at moms to see the need for every single person to carry the message of the gospel in the season of life they have found themselves. Their training has helped me to think outside the box in how I can disciple not only my own children, but their friends, and the others I interact with on a daily basis."

Andrea Boyd
Stay at home mother of three, Portland, OR

"I've seen the leaders of The Table Network create a culture of life change, that is powerful and transformative. They are leaders who take seriously what Jesus said to do. They are going into their world to make disciples who make disciples, and the Father is using this powerful tribe of leaders and churches."

Dan Grider
Founder and Director, Ignite Church Network

"With all the responsibilities that come with being on staff at a mega church, I found little time to engage the people around me who were uninterested in the church. The Table Network has helped me and my family re-engage our call to make disciples in the harvest, and there, see a new church family form that's doing the same."

Bill Vecchio
Pastor/Planter, Fort Myers Community Church

"I absolutely resonate with how The Table Network has reclaimed, from the Scriptures, a simple approach to reaching those who have no intention in attending a church service. I've personally seen how this network raises up everyday disciples to make disciples in everyday common places. I am no different than my neighbors. Broken. Messy. Yet I know I'm loved by God in Christ. This is the good news, and the mission is the freeing call to share this, as we go, with those we love and live among."

James Purrazzo
Firefighter/Paramedic &
Leader of The Table Chicago/Bridgeport

"Slow Down is an insightful work for anyone committed to Jesus' words in the Great Commission. It provides a step-by-step approach to engaging those in your world with the gospel. The Table Network is an important resource to churches and Christians alike looking for a "how to" focused on engaging their friends, neighbors and co-workers with the gospel and seeing them come to faith in Jesus Christ."

Rick Dunn
Executive Director, Gateway Leadership Initiative

SLOW DOWN

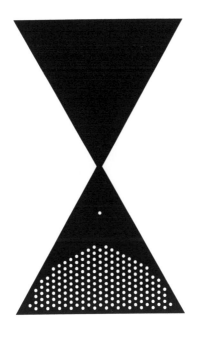

Russ Johnson
Gino Curcuruto
Tony Sorci

SLOW DOWN

Produced by Table Network Resources
www.thetablenetwork.com

Published by Missional Challenge Publishing
www.missionalchallenge.com

PUBLISHING

Design/Cover: Tony Sorci

ISBN-13: 978-1-939921-84-0

This book is dedicated to the misfits.

CONTENTS

INTRODUCTION

If you peak into the conversation concerning the spiritual decay of our time, you will inevitably be hit with a crowd calling for the church to return to its mission of "making disciples." You will also most likely find some of the most fundamental truths of humanity missing from the push for people to "Go" as Jesus said:

- We naturally extend to others what we enjoy.

- We can only enjoy what we experience.

To forget this ancient connection, between what we experience and what we then extend to others, leads to the constant call for the latter while ignoring the former. A call that has profound implications on the number of people who have been burnt and burnt out in the name of the *Great Commission.*

As a leader who was once well-versed in this sincere tyranny, God used two things I love in 2013, movies and meals, to reveal this "forgotten" connection. I can remember the moment when it dawned on me how I've never seen the credits roll with a plea to "go tell others about this film," nor have I ever left a restaurant with a request from the chef to "please spread the word."

Why?

Because both parties focus on providing the opportunity to experience something of real value, knowing that if we enjoy it, we will naturally extend this good to others.

This connection is timeless; it can be found in every facet of life. But as those who love to use the law of "what should be" to measure performance, map our way forward, and manage progress... oh how easy it is to forget. Like those who are freshly invigorated with the sense of success found in building ships to sail the missional seas, we somehow fail to keep in mind that we have no ability to fashion the wind. Which is perhaps why we need to be reminded often that it's God who is at work, it is we who have been invited to walk in Him, and it's what we do as His Church that fosters the opportunity for others to experience the freedom and family found at Jesus' table.

When I made this connection, it became abundantly clear how more missional pleas from the platform will never sustain a movement of discipleship, especially in a day where the gospel isn't news for many and most are uninterested in attending anything the church offers.

We need another way forward, another way of being the church that breeds the natural enjoyment and extension of the freedom and family found at the table Jesus has prepared.

To this end, I stopped looking for new answers to the same questions, and instead started asking some new ones:

- How do we get the message of freedom, this scandalous invitation of Jesus to come dine with Him at the table of rest, to an exhausted world longing for peace?

- How do we put the medium of family— the church itself—back into the hands of everyday people around the simplicity of good food, Good News and good conversation?

- How do we help those who long to enjoy

and extend this message and medium find rest, slow down, and make disciples amongst those outside the church?

This short book is a simple look at how a timeless approach to these questions is resonating among those in the church who long for more, as well as those who are uninterested in the norm.

By design, this book won't answer all the questions that will surface; it's not intended to provide all the answers. Our aim here is only to begin (or continue) a much-needed conversation about what it tangibly looks like for the church to provide everyone with the opportunity to experience the freedom and family found at the table Jesus has prepared.

Russ Johnson
Founder, *The Table Network*

1

WHAT ABOUT BOB(S)?

A MODERN DAY DILEMMA

Bob is an everyday guy with a common story. He made it out of the house alive, took on debt, juggled the act of play and work through college, found Jesus, landed a job, scraped pennies together for an apartment, soaked up all his city had to offer, met the right girl, and started a family.

At his core, when the dust settles from the intense push at work and the endless pull of life in the 21st Century, Bob longs for just a few things: to see Jesus bring about real change to his life, to what he believes and experiences on a daily basis; to see Jesus bring change to what his wife and daughter believe and how they live in relationship to God and others; and Bob longs to see Jesus awaken his friends and neighbors and co-workers to His love and grace so they too may know Him.

With a heart for these things, Bob joined a large church. He's a faithful giver, attender, and an active part of a small group with his family. Check one.

As someone who believes in giving his time and talents to the church, Bob serves with his wife in the kids ministry once a month, as well heading up the Sunday morning Welcome Team. Check two.

Lately though, Bob's friends have weighed heavy on his mind, one of whom is Vicky. He wants them to experience the freedom and family found at the table Jesus has prepared. And in the hope to see this happen, he expends great effort to make his church a place his friends would want to visit. Month after month, Bob looks for the perfect opportunity to invite Vicky to something she'd be interested in attending. Getting Vicky to a church event has become his focus, his mission.

There's just one problem: no matter what his church seems to do, most of Bob's friends are not interested in attending any of the services they offer, or the smaller missional communities that meet during the week. So Bob begins thinking about what an expression of the church could look like that is conducive to the interests, rhythms, and even learning styles of his friends outside the church.

Creating this expression though is quickly met with a few dilemmas:

First, Bob's experience within the church tells him that the idea of creating something for his friends outside the church is simply out of his reach. To be a church, in his mind and the minds of others, requires a building to house a large crowd, a band to lead worship, volunteers for all the ministries, time in the week to lead all these efforts, and the money to pull it off. Without a building and a Sunday service, Bob has been told that his church will never have any credibility. This view not only moves the idea of creating a new church out of his grasp, but also out of his interest. Bob has a good job. He's not interested in leaving it to start a new church with all it would demand.

Second, Bob's experience within the church tells him that well-crafted sermons and specific programs are needed for people to grow in their Christian walk. He's been told: 1) "Your daughter really needs a vibrant kids ministry if you want to see her grow up in the faith, love the church, and have all the needed experiences that come with it." 2) "The discipleship and growth of you, your wife, and your friends who aren't interested in the church will be limited at best without the weekly presentations and programs of a conventional church structure."

Lastly, Bob's experience within the church tells him that a formal education, through an accredited Bible college or seminary, is needed in order for Bob to be a leader/pastor/elder who can truly guide a church family and teach sound doctrine. Without this formal education under his belt, Bob has been told that he will be unqualified for the role and responsibilities of pastoral leadership.

And so, Bob stays in the current system. His story isn't unique. In fact, Bob's story represents hundreds of people we have met and discipled across the West who range from millennials to retirees, creatives to entrepreneurs, church leaders to industry leaders.

Perhaps you're in his shoes right now?

Which is why it's a good idea to stop and ask ourselves a few questions (in light of the paradigm Bob holds about the church, discipleship, and leadership) to perhaps see something we may otherwise be missing:

- From a practical point of view, when 35% of people age 15-30 (highest percentage in U.S. history) want nothing to do with any form of spirituality, and upwards of 70% of the population isn't interested in attending a church service of any kind, does it matter how great the church service is if people aren't looking for one? And from a Biblical point of view, can Bob not see a new church family gather in simple ways around the table in his home when it appears this is what the church families did throughout the New Testament?

- Christianity is a life of *"faith, hope, and love,"* not "law, knowledge, and performance" (1 Cor 13). Knowing this life is caught more than taught; Jesus used a Hebraic teaching style that invited people to come act their way into a new way of thinking. If this is true, then why is it so common in our day to think change, the very thing we all long for, happens best through information dissemination programs that are void of the faith and

5

practice seen in the ways Jesus discipled others?

- Throughout the New Testament we see the church as a multiplying movement primarily led by everyday and mostly unnamed people. In a time when we need not just thousands of new church families, but millions, to meet every man, woman, and child where they are, should our primary means for developing leaders to start these new churches be foreign to the in-house, local context, along-the-way, need-driven approach of the New Testament church?

At the heart of the change you want to experience in your life, the life of your family and the lives of your friends like Vicky, you may need to make some mental shifts concerning the nature of the church and discipleship. You may also need to be equipped to walk in this nature as you seek to establish the framework needed to champion gospel movement in the everyday.

The Table Network seeks to empower you, and millions like you, with the resources and relationships needed to see those shifts take shape throughout your life and context. And as a network with many pastors who at one time didn't know how to identify, empower, and release the Bob's within their congregation, we seek to serve Bob's pastor as well. (See Appendix 2.)

To move forward into what could be... we have found it best to first look backward.

We need to take a closer look at the Scriptures.

It is there we discover another way.

2

PAUL'S PERSPECTIVE

*A NEW TESTAMENT STORY
OF SLOWING DOWN*

How did the early church move from a small group of 120 misfits gathered in an upper room to reaching nearly 65% of the Roman Empire within just 300 years?

What did they believe?

How did they live and love?

As we look to these questions in hopes to experience this kind of movement in both our lives and our lifetime, it's good to avoid some of the hype swirling and be reminded of what's been right under our nose all along. Richard Niebuhr said it well:

"The great Christian revolutions came not by the discovery of something that was not known before, but rather when someone takes radically something that was always there."

So, let's look back at the beliefs and behaviors of these early Christians, and one in particular...the Apostle Paul.

While the early Church was forming, a young man named Saul, a Pharisee, was rising to prominence. Saul opposed all who followed Jesus and had a mission to wipe them out. Violently. This hatred for these early Christ followers was driven by a message that flew right in the face of everything Saul thought was right about God and serving Him. In short, Saul's message was one of keeping the Law while this early church proclaimed the Messiah had lived, died, and rose again fulfilling the Law for all who believed. To be blunt, Saul not only opposed these Christians, he tried to destroy them. He actively sought to thwart their efforts to spread their message by killing them. Ironically, in Saul's pursuit of Christians, he was being pursued by Jesus. And Jesus would change Saul's mission and message dramatically! (See Galatians 1:11-16)

After Jesus literally interrupted Saul's

mission on the road to Damascus, Saul was given a new identity in Christ. Saul became aware of the folly of his previous mission to stop Christians and received the hope of his new mission to walk with Jesus and show others how to do the same. With this radical shift in the message and the mission, Saul, who also became known as Paul, was sent as an ambassador on behalf of Jesus.

Paul's New Mission, Message, and Medium

Along with Paul's new mission, that is, God's mission, he proclaimed a new message. No longer was obedience to the Law the pathway to life. Paul now proclaimed the message of Good News... attempting to uphold the Law leads to recognition of your inability to do so. Rather than pretending, faking, or lowering the standard, we proclaim our failure — our utter inability to measure up to God's perfect standards for righteousness. But this is only part of the Good News... Jesus fulfilled the Law on our behalf and now through faith, His perfection is ours. His life is your life and you are free! Contrary to the idea that we all have a life that we need to give over to the Lordship of Jesus, the Scriptures teach us that Jesus is life. To awaken to life in Him you need only admit your death. No more faking it. No more boasting. Your pathway to life is admitting your death and receiving Jesus' life, death, and resurrection by faith. This is a message of freedom. This is good news for the world.

Paul, now sent and empowered by the Holy Spirit, set out on this mission to make disciples through walking in and sharing this message of freedom. Paul and his team journeyed through many different parts of the known world. While he shared the same message, he found that in order for people to learn how to walk by faith in the freedom Christ has given, the medium through which it was transmitted required flexibility. The message stayed the same, but the medium was free to adapt to new contexts. Whether it was through Lydia, the seller of purple, or the Philippian jailer, it seemed a common practice for Paul and the other apostles to focus on planting the gospel among and through families or webs of relationship. (See Acts 10; 16:11-15; 16:25-40)

- What medium could allow a group of people to walk with Jesus and show others to do the same?

- What medium would allow those within a group to proclaim this message of freedom to one another and to those outside the group?

• And how can this same medium be adaptable to allow for differences in the context in which these people lived?

When you consider it, it is somewhat challenging to find a medium "sticky" enough for people to want to walk in yet flexible enough to allow for cultural and contextual differences. It appears that Paul found a perfect medium. It is one demonstrated throughout the New Testament. The medium that is conducive to sharing the message of freedom through the lens of any context is family. By family we mean, a group of people hungry to follow Jesus together. Families are made up of all kinds of people — elderly, kids, couples, singles, widows, young professionals, and college students. God's family is diverse and inclusive!

Throughout the Scriptures we see references to the church as God's family. In 1 Corinthians 12:27, the church is referred to as *"the body of Christ"* in the world. One family united to Jesus and one another. One family made up of millions of expressions gathering and scattering. It's not something we do or build, it's simply who we are.

One of the beautiful things about the way the apostles spread the message of freedom through the medium of family is that most people did not need to dramatically change their life or add new things to their routines in order to be discipled or make new disciples. Walking as a disciple didn't require people to create more margin (time), only to live intentionally in what they were already doing. Paul called people to proclaim the Good News where they lived as the body (family of God); all members of the family are ministers (2 Cor 5). The gatherings of the church took place over everyday meals (no additional time required) and mission occurred in everyday living ("as you are going" Matt. 28:19).

The shift came not so much in what the people were doing — they were already doing many of these things. The shift was not in their doing but in their "being." It was a shift in their identity that led them to live differently within the same rhythms of life that they already experienced. The medium of family created margin for disciple-making because nothing was added to what they were doing.

As this message of freedom (the gospel) was "planted" in the hearts of people, new families begin to form and take shape in their context. And as families quickly became the medium through which this mission spread, more people began to form new Spirit-empowered families. Paul knew that the mission was to see freedom announced through the medium of families who mobilize new families through this process. He saw it happen in his time. But how did Paul see the gospel continue to get planted into the hearts of new people beyond the initial families he saw form? Paul seemed to focus on equipping mobilizers (leaders) to care for and multiply the number of families in a community or region.

"And he gave the apostles, the prophets, the evangelists, the shepherds and teachers, to equip the saints for the work of ministry, for building up the body of Christ, until we all attain to the unity of the faith and of the knowledge of the Son of God, to mature manhood." (Ephesians 4:11-13a)

Paul gave much of his time to discipleship and care of the people who would lead in equipping and mobilizing others for the work of ministry. These leaders became mobilizers for the mission. When mobilizers are released, disciples are made and sent out to love, disciple, and see new families form. This is what Paul saw and why he poured into leaders.

By proclaiming a message of freedom through the medium of family, the normal rhythms of life became the work of the mission. No additional margin was needed. As Paul was going along the way, he discipled others and taught them to do the same, creating mobilizers. This resulted in movement, rapid spread of the gospel, throughout the known world. In learning from Paul's story, it is clear that the message and medium championed movement because it provided margin for its people and the mobilizers needed to equip them to disciple.

Simply put, a message worth sharing, shared through a medium people were already living in (family) did not require more "to dos" for the members of the family or the leaders (mobilizers), and thus affording people margin to actually enter into the mission of God.

So we ask, "In a day when the gospel isn't 'news' to many and most are uninterested in attending a church gathering, what would it look like to see Paul's approach to discipleship happen in our current context?" We think the Apostle Paul's story has much to teach all of us today, particularly in how to see the mission result in movement.

What if we returned to a reckless message of freedom, lived through a loving medium of family in the everyday, affording all members and mobilizers the margin needed for movement to result?

At The Table Network, we believe these ancient truths are there to be reclaimed in our current times.

3

THE FREEDOM
TO SLOW DOWN

*WHY YOU CAN STOP FOCUSING
SO MUCH ON YOU*

It seems counterintuitive to look at the tension Bob is facing about change in his life, his family's life, and the life of his friends outside the church, and say to him, "You need to slow down if you want to see that dream move from a thought in your head to a reality in your midst."

So welcome to one of the many paradoxes of the gospel.

Perhaps one of the best places to view this

paradox is in the story we often refer to as: The Good Samaritan. If anything unveils the root reason why Bob can slow down to love and disciple others, it's this story from Jesus. Simon Sinek is right...we should always start with the "why."

We find the parable recorded in Luke 10:25-37, and the name we have given it is often used for hospitals, justice ministries, and as the battle cry for those staring down the many racial divides, educational gaps, refugee crisis, and many other injustices. These are real issues where we want to see what is good and right have its full effect.

But, in further study of this passage, we find, like the disciples who spent years with Jesus, that we may have missed a deeper meaning to what Jesus is declaring in this ancient parable. In fact, we may have missed the very connection He's making between what we want to see come to fruition in our world and how we actually arrive at this desired destination.

The story begins with Jesus' encounter with a lawyer, *"For behold, a lawyer stood up to put him* (Jesus) *to the test,"* (Luke 10:25). This is a man, mind you, who was an expert in the Jewish Law. To say he had the Law of God and all its many facets (613 commands) memorized would not be an overstatement. From what we can tell, he apparently has heard about Jesus from others, has gone to listen to Jesus, and in his observation felt there is a serious divide between what God has declared in the Law and what Jesus is teaching.

So, right out of the gate, the lawyer begins his onslaught with one simple question: *"Teacher, what shall I do to inherit eternal life?"* (vs 25)

It's a simple, straightforward question, and with death being a destiny awaiting us all, a very relevant question. Jesus, as a skilled teacher, begins the process of answering the lawyer's question by asking him a question, *"What is written in the Law? How do you read it?"* (vs 26)

Ready to share his immense knowledge of the Law at a moment's notice, the lawyer responds, *"You shall love the Lord your God with all your heart and with all your soul and with all your strength and with all your mind, and your neighbor as yourself."* (vs 27)

Ding. Ding. Ding. *"You have answered correctly,"* Jesus said. *"Do this, and you will live."* (vs 28)

You could have heard a pin drop as the lawyer was assured that Jesus' beliefs about the Law and his teachings on eternal life were in line with what God had declared. But instead of being satisfied with Jesus' answer, an eerie look comes across his face as he quickly and quietly realizes: "According to the Scriptures, If I 'do this,' this very essence of the Law, this act of loving God with everything I am and loving my neighbor in the same degree that I love myself...then I 'will live.'"

Most of us read this and think, "Alright. A clear to do list. I got this. Thank you, Jesus!" But for the lawyer here, this wasn't a moment of gratitude... it was a moment of sheer panic.

As a lawyer, he knew better than anyone else in his day how the perfect Law to *"love God with all"* of your being and to *"love your neighbor as yourself"* is only done, only met, only fulfilled, if it is done with perfection. Yes, righteousness, "rightness," is what we need to live in the presence of a holy God. There is no such thing as imperfect obedience.

The very Law the lawyer had just used to justify himself incriminated himself.

So rather than face the reality of his need and his inability to meet it, *"he, desiring to justify himself, said to Jesus, 'And who is my neighbor?'"* (vs 29)

The question is an escape tactic, a back-peddle ploy rooted in a man-made spin on the Law, aimed at helping the lawyer get around the demands of loving God and his neighbor with perfection. In response to this move, Jesus goes into a story of a man who was traveling on a long stretch of dangerous, isolated terrain from *"Jerusalem to Jericho"* where he *"fell among robbers, who stripped him and beat him and departed, leaving him half dead."* Scene 1 of the opening act is set with a Jewish man (for only he would have been traveling from this direction) who is broken and desperately in need of someone outside of himself to save him.

Jesus then goes on and says, *"a priest was going down that road, and when he saw him he passed by on the other side,"* followed by a *"Levite"* who took this same course of action (vs 31-32). With scene 2, two new characters are added to the plot, one representing the Law of Moses and the other its role in the world. Both are naturally good, informative, and even directive, but neither have any ability to actually bring change to the human heart. Like a mirror, the Law can reveal the dirt on your face. Amen. However, rubbing your face on a mirror will never make it clean.

So here you have two men who, in keeping with the ceremonial law, abstain from helping someone who is bleeding and dying.

In other words, the Law doesn't lead to life because the Law doesn't lead to love.

Knowing this, Jesus brings the story to its climax as He says that a *"Samaritan,"* the sworn enemy of the Jewish people, unlike the Priest and Levite... *"when he saw him, ...had compassion."* Jesus went on to spell out what this loving compassion looked like as the Samaritan *"bound up his wounds, ...set him on his own animal and brought him to an inn to take care of him."* Jesus then showed them what loving generosity looks like as this Samaritan covered the stranger's medical expenses, paying the innkeeper to take care of him until he returned (vs 33-35). Think of the medical cost today entailed in nursing someone to health who is at the point of death. The estimate in today's setting can be upwards of an entire year's salary.

With the full scenario and each character's role in view, Jesus moves to the heart of the lawyer's question and asks: *"Which of these three, do you think, proved to be a neighbor to the man who fell among the robbers?"* (vs 36). In other words, in light of the Law you quoted just a minute ago about what you need to do to inherit eternal life, the question isn't "Who is your neighbor?" but rather "What kind of neighbor are you?" The lawyer answers, *"the one who showed him mercy."* And with the lawyer's ploy exposed, Jesus makes sure his original question is clearly answered: *"You go, and do likewise."* (vs 37)

The parable is pure genius.

Jesus uses a story about a man who is desperately in need of someone else to save him after being *"beaten half dead"*...a guy the lawyer refuses to identify with, who was loved by a *"Samaritan"*...someone the lawyer will not identify with, to show him what he *"must do to inherit eternal life"*...a task he cannot identify with.

And perhaps that is the point.

With the beliefs most likely held by the lawyer in regard to what is wrong with the world and what the solutions are to fix it, he was looking for a Messiah who was coming to make the world straighten up and fly right, not *"the Lamb of God"* who is slain to take *"away the sins of the world"* (Jn. 1:29). It's the same song and dance with everyone in Jesus' context, including the disciples who, prior to the telling of this parable, were asking Jesus about sending down fire on a Samaritan village for refusing him a place to stay. So, as people who were thinking they needed a guide rather than a Savior, they would naturally see themselves as the Samaritan in Jesus' story, not the helpless man on the side of the road.

Ironically, only in recognizing our death, our inability to live out the demands of the law with our righteousness of *"filthy rags,"* will we ever cling to the only One who's in the resurrection business. (Isaiah 64:6)

It is Jesus, and Jesus alone, who fulfills the Law and *"inherits eternal life."* By God's grace, He has announced that His Father's dealings with the sin problem of our world are *"finished,"* forgiven. (John 19) By God's grace, His *"righteousness"* has been attributed to all who believe (Rom 3-4; Eph 2:8-10). And by God's grace, *"all things,"* as in everything that feels lost from our acts of pride, greed, fear, hatred, racism, sexism, manipulation, abuse, theft, lying... *"has been reconciled"* in the life, death, and resurrection of the one who made us, loved us, forgave us, and sustains us all. (Col 1:15-20)

In Jesus, reality has undergone a major shift.

We need nothing else...except to believe in

the One who's made this life-changing news a reality.

Believing we stand complete in Jesus is what allows us the freedom to look at the purpose of the Law, this beautiful picture of love for God and others, not as a to-do list to obtain the holiness the Law demands, but as a picture of what harmony with God and others truly looks like. This by no means removes the call on our lives to what is good and worthy of pursuit; it just changes the posture of our pursuit as the Law, this *"ministry of death,"* reveals the impossible feat of us ever walking in our own righteousness. (2 Cor 3:1-9) It's a journey, marked not by determined action, but rather complete dependence on Jesus who is our salvation and sanctification. (Heb 10:13)

Believing we stand complete in Jesus is what allows us the freedom to die to the project of self, the tyranny of more, and the need to posture ourselves as someone who has it together. The independent life, apart from Him who is *"life,"* is a myth. (Jn 14:6; Gal 2:20) We are completely *"hidden"* in Him. (Col 3) There are no levels in the kingdom, no ladders to climb in hopes to reach your next breakthrough... just a Savior to dwell in. So you're free to stop giving away all of your limited margin to church programs centered around your growth, and like the disciples, run with Jesus as He ministers to those outside - an actual place of need that drives your dependence and discipleship.

Lastly, believing that we stand complete in Jesus is what allows us the freedom to stop racking our brains in search of the magic bullet to help us build the church. Jesus said, *"I will build My church,"* it's not something we do. (Matt 16:18) It is easy to lose sight of this promise when we mistakenly place this task upon ourselves or when we face trials, fail, and feel defeated. Just as it's easy to forget how the early church was a vast movement that brought the news of Jesus to much of the known world with only one resource: His Spirit. No copy of the Scriptures for everyone to study, no seminaries, no large Sunday venues, just the Spirit at work through everyday people who had been *"given the ministry of reconciliation"* (2 Cor 5).

Knowing what He would accomplish on the cross, Jesus slowed down to disciple others.

Knowing what He has accomplished on the cross, we can slow down to disciple others as He works in us, with us, without us, and even in spite of us.

Such good news for the lawyer in us all.

4

THE NEED TO SLOW DOWN

WHAT "MAKING DISCIPLES" ACTUALLY MEANS

With the overwhelming amount of resources designed to help you take action in the world of making disciples, we have found very few begin with the biblical truth of slowing down with and like Jesus.

Perhaps that makes us standout? We don't really know, nor do we claim to have created this idea. We just know the mission Jesus gave us was to: *"Go therefore and make disciples."* (Matt 28:19) The disciples learned this in a unique way. And at the heart of this is the concept of slowing down. Let us explain.

The disciples were slow to understand (as we all are) that God's kingdom was never of the strong-arm variety. These men thought Jesus' kingdom was a physical kingdom with walls (and Jewish people safely inside those walls) and an army built for war to secure their safety and autonomy. They also thought Jesus was the king who would gather such an army to overcome their Roman oppressors and establish such a kingdom. They really, truly believed this. This idea of a king and kingdom was ingrained in them. It was all they knew.

How crushing it must have been to watch Jesus die at the hands of the superpower He was supposed to overthrow? Just devastating. The dream is over. Dejection. Depression. On to the next potential king.

It would only be three days later this dead dream would rise along with Jesus literally rising from the dead. The disciples had to have been thinking they'd be heading into battle with a Messiah who can't die. His kingdom would truly have no end, they thought. And yet, forty days go by (Acts 1:3) where Jesus had talked a ton about His kingdom, but no army was formed, and no plans were made to establish this kingdom.

The disciples were left wondering when they were actually going to get on with it (Acts 1:6) and some, toward the end, were even doubting (Matthew 28:17).

What was the point of all this? Why die? Why come back? What are you doing, Jesus? What role do we play? These are the questions (doubts you might say) going through their heads and hearts. A confusing and uncertain time for the guys who thought they would be high-ranking officers in Jesus' military.

Into all this doubting, Jesus spoke these words recorded in Matthew 28:19-20...

> *"Go therefore and make disciples of all nations, baptizing them in the name of the Father and of the Son and of the Holy Spirit, teaching them to observe all that I have commanded you. And behold, I am with you always, to the end of the age."*

The mission here had nothing to do with a large military, but everything to do with all the little moments Jesus spent slowing down with these eleven: every conversation as they walked on the road, every meal, every intense conversation around a fire at night, every parable, every prayer, every mission He sent them on, every moment they observed Jesus love, extend grace, heal, teach, and refute the religious community.

Three years of slowing down with Jesus was all they needed to be equipped for the slow journey of disciple-making Jesus called them to.

Like these guys, we believe all who have been *"reconciled"* to God have been given *"the ministry of reconciliation,"* and commissioned by Jesus to, *"go and make disciples."* (2 Cor 5:18; Matt 28:19) And as we have taken steps to reclaim these truths in our time, we have found value not only in looking at the details surrounding Jesus' words in Matthew 28, but also looking into what it looks like practically to make disciples in the postmodern/post-Christian society we find ourselves in.

Before we take any steps toward living out this call, we want to encourage you to pause and consider what Jesus is calling us to do. Often our assumptions about the Great Commission lead to us feeling overwhelmed and burdened. So much for that easy yoke and light burden, right? (Matt 11:30). But contrary to our feelings, Jesus is not contradicting His offer of an easy yoke and light burden when He calls us to *"go therefore and make disciples."* A closer look at the Great Commission will reveal this to be a beautiful, freeing truth we so desperately need.

Let us explain.

The first thing Bible scholars will tell you is when you encounter the word, *"therefore"* you need to ask yourself the question, "What is 'therefore' there for?" The answer is in the preceding verse where Jesus reminds his "twelve" disciples that all authority is given to Him in heaven and on earth. Pushing it further, He made His chosen ones stewards of that dominion and authority, and on that basis authorized them and their mission to disciple.

Although Jesus' commission is agreed to be paramount, there is confusion on exactly what He commissioned His followers to do. *"Go therefore and make disciples of all nations"* can be read a couple different ways. The standard approach has a missionary bent towards being sent out to other nations in order to make disciples. However, there are several reasons why this reading is problematic. A clearer understanding of this passage will help us see the mission and being a missionary as something for both here and other nations.

The difficulty in seeing this from the passage is largely because two verbs are present: *'go'* and *'make disciples'*.

Let's start with *'go'*. (Brace yourself; this is a bit of grammar talk.) Verbs come in two common forms: infinitive and participle. So for our example, it would be either 'go' (infinitive) or 'going' (participle). Most Bible translations render the word as 'go', although the Greek word in the original text is a participle. It should be translated 'going' or 'as you are going.'

The other issue is with *'make disciples'*, and this is more of a theological issue. If someone is commanded to make disciples, the implication is that it is in their power to make it happen. However, we know from Scripture that the One who makes disciples is God Himself; we simply point people to Him. The resolve here, in light of all Jesus' teachings, is to use the verb 'disciple' (as in, "I disciple Joe"). Although God is the one who makes disciples, the commission here to disciple people is the imperative. "Go disciple people!"

By putting both of these ideas together, the rendering of the text becomes, "Therefore, as you are going, disciple people of all nations, baptizing them..."

With this reading, the pressure of a command is lifted and replaced with the natural organic flow of moving through life and watching for the Holy Spirit opportunity to DISCIPLE! This translation lifts off the sense of compartmentalization of work, family, and ministry, and weaves the mission of discipling others to Jesus (unbelievers) or in Jesus (believers) through all of life in an organic way.

In light of the meaning unveiled in the words of Jesus in Matthew 28, and the discipleship efforts we see from Him and others throughout the New Testament, we believe discipleship is best defined as "spiritual conversations as you go". Since you can't actually convert or change anyone, the pressure is off you to try to make that happen. You are free to slow down with people, walk through life with them while you have spiritual conversations along the way.

What do these "spiritual conversations" look like? What form of ministry do you need to create to carry them out?

It would be foolish of us to assume we can tell you the exact answer because we don't know the people you are discipling to Jesus. However, we do see five functions of discipleship in the life of Jesus, functions we have seen within spiritual conversations that occur throughout all contexts. We have also seen how these five functions are all undergirded by trust in the Spirit to bear fruit.

Knowing how to disciple someone is important, but so is knowing that the opportunity is lost quickly if you aren't trusting the Spirit to bear fruit in their lives when and how He chooses. It's with this firm foundation of trust we see these five functions of discipleship:

- **Presence** with the people in our lives.

- **Listening** to the people we are discipling.

- **Sharing** the person and promises of Jesus in light of where they are.

- **Inviting** people to step into where God is leading them.

- **Teaching** people to wait, watch, and walk in the fruit where the Spirit is at work.

We will look a little closer at each of these five functions in the next chapter. Before we do, let's pause and consider again why we must slow down. We could sum it up like this: By God's grace, everyone who has awakened to Jesus has simultaneously been *"given the ministry of reconciliation,"* and commissioned by Jesus to, *"go therefore and make disciples..."*

(Matt 28:19-20 and 2 Cor 5:18).

Like the brothers and sisters that have gone before us, we believe the gospel spreads to every nook and cranny of society through discipleship in the hands of each and every believer. This journey of discipleship is a process of spiritual conversations over time. Therefore, to enter in to relationship, to actually disciple someone to walk with Jesus, we will need to slow down with him or her.

Now on to the "how."

5

THE ART OF
SLOWING DOWN

*DISCIPLESHIP AT THE
SPEED OF LIFE*

We have described discipleship as spiritual conversations as you go through life with others. Also, we have emphasized that you get to slow down with others in order to have these conversations with others. While the content of these spiritual conversations will largely be shaped by the stories of the people you are discipling, we believe there are five functions, timeless, ancient functions you can say, that consistently and repeatedly occur. These five functions are: being present, listening, sharing, inviting, and teaching.

Consider these five functions as a framework (rather than rules) as you disciple others.

PRESENCE

While it may seem redundant to say we should be present with the people we are discipling, we believe it is worth emphasizing. Intentionally showing up in people's lives is an often-overlooked function of discipleship. *"The Word became flesh and dwelled among us"* (John 1) is not merely a poetic turn of phrase, but rather a demonstration of the incarnational and intentional love of Jesus. Because we live in Him (Gal. 2:20), we are ambassadors of Jesus (2 Cor 5:20) who incarnate among the people in our lives. We are present among people. We intentionally show up for their sake: ready, willing, and able to listen to them, serve them, and proclaim good news.

Discipleship begins with relationship, and relationships begin by being present in someone's life. Sure, you may have "accidentally" met your future spouse on a "chance" meeting, but you didn't get to know one another by accident. You intentionally made time to be around each other and be available for one another. Now we aren't saying that discipleship is like dating, merely drawing the similarity between how relationships begin and how discipleship begins the same way.

What might this look like? We have experienced and hear about people intentionally being present in the lives of co-workers, baristas, classmates, bus drivers, neighbors, etc. One of our leaders intentionally joined a running group for men coming out of addiction. By just showing up a few days a week, he has seen some fantastic relationships form. The guys grow in trust because this leader is consistent in being present.

The gospel frees us to intentionally seek others without needing others. Because we are fully loved, adopted, approved, and accepted in Jesus, we can be present in the lives of others without needing a "return on the investment." By putting on Jesus and dwelling among others, we have a valuable and loving presence in the lives of those around us. Some will notice and grow in trust, giving us an opportunity to listen to them and get to know their story. No strings attached.

LISTENING

In a world where everyone loves to share and few like to listen, those who slow down with others so they can hear their stories will find out where people are in life, what they're celebrating, and what they're struggling with in life. Because adults learn on a need-to-know basis, there's simply no way to disciple someone from where they are if you don't first know where they are and what they desire to know.

Tragically, most of us, if we're honest, are well versed in proclaiming truth and quite immature as listeners. Whether our desire to share truth comes from a heart of love (a good thing) or a desire to prove ourselves (a sinful thing), often the effect on the hearer is the same -- "These Christians don't really understand me, and I don't understand why Jesus is relevant to me." (Or something similar).

In our zeal to see people "repent and believe", we fail to listen to what their story is about. We miss hearing what their belief is and what they trust in, what they hope in, what they truly worship. Please hear us carefully. We are not advocating people remain in the beliefs and behaviors keeping them at arm's length from Jesus or that you avoid speaking truth. We are urging all of us to consider how Jesus often listened to the desires of people's hearts, He heard their story, and spoke truth in light of that.

Consider the woman at the well (John 4). While the story is well known by most Christians, the practice of Jesus may seem foreign to how we share the gospel. For many of us, we would have been more comfortable with the story going something like this:

Jesus approaches the woman at the well. He knows that for her to be out fetching water at this odd time of day, she must be an outcast from society. Probably, a someone who has suffered abuse and is deeply entrenched in sin. Assuming this, Jesus walks up to the woman and says, "Woman. Something is obviously wrong. People don't come out to get water from this well this late in the day. Well, unless they are trying not to be seen. It is your sin that keeps you in shame and hiding. If you would receive the free gift I am offering, you would be free from what is destroying your life."

We realize the above retelling is a paraphrase. However, the truth in this retelling is still present in the "words" of Jesus. Yes, the woman was suffering in her unbelief. Yes, she felt shame and disconnect from society. And yes, she needed the salvation Jesus would offer in Himself. So why did Jesus waste time asking her questions instead of just getting to the point? We think the answer to this question is why listening is a valuable function in discipleship.

Adults learn on a need-to-know basis. Just because something is true doesn't mean it is going to be valuable or memorable for someone. Being told you're a sinner and need a savior isn't important if you don't actually believe you need rescue! Being offered the free gift of life in Jesus is of no consequence if you still believe there is such a thing as an independent life across the street from Him who is life Himself (John 14:6; Col 1:15-20).

In the story of the Samaritan woman at the well, Jesus gives us an amazing lesson on listening. He doesn't begin with sharing truth but begins a conversation and listens to her. In doing so, He reveals her true reality. This unveiling of truth isn't just revealed to Jesus (He seems to already know something about her), but it is revealed to the woman as well. As she shares she hears, and upon hearing, her need is apparent. Now she is ready to learn.

Since adults learn on a need-to-know basis, listening is a great place to start.

SHARING

Once someone has shared an aspect of their story with you, then you have the opportunity not to preach at them, but instead to share a part of your story that connects with theirs. It's here people are able to see you're just like them. It's here you can share what God has shown and taught you in light of the topic on the table. And it's here those who aren't ready for "meat" (a look at the Scriptures), are discipled with "milk" (stories of how you have been shaped by the Person and promises of Jesus).

The posture (for want of a better word) of sharing from a common need is so refreshing. Rather than telling people how messed up they are and how you have answers for them, sharing your story in light of theirs, levels the playing field. You're not a hero here to save them. In fact, you're just like them, a broken person desperately in need of rescue from the Savior. Your story isn't that Jesus just improved a generally decent person. No! Your story is that Jesus replaced a hell-bent broken person who thought they could manage right and wrong apart from their Creator. And isn't that everyone's story?

By sharing our common brokenness and shared need, we can then introduce Jesus in a way that is meaningful. It is in our weakness that Jesus is seen as the hero that He is. There's only One in the winner's circle.

For example, I (Gino) often hear people share of their deep sense of needing to prove themselves. Whether it's through excelling in school, getting a promotion at work, or having the finest sneakers, we have a desire to show our value and worth through achievements. One such discussion was with a friend Roger (not his real name). Roger grew up in a difficult, abusive home. He was physically and emotionally abused and remembers as a young man feeling, "if there is a God, He doesn't love me."

Roger wanted so much to not repeat the abuse of his past with his children, so much so that he prided himself on all the things he was able to provide for his kids and worked very hard to do so. Yet, Roger wasn't living in the freedom of the gospel. He was constantly trying to prove that he was a better parent than he had AND to prove that he was good enough to be valued by the same people who he wanted nothing to do with. Can you relate?

As Roger and I got to know each other, shared meals and conversation together, I was able to share some of my own story with him. I told him something like this:

"Roger, my story isn't the same as yours. I wasn't abused in the same way you were. My parents always tried to care for me and were affectionate. Yet, I feel I can relate to you in needing to show that I am significant or worthy. You see, when I was about 11 years old, my parents got divorced and life wasn't the same for me. Shortly after that, we moved a long distance from my dad and I really didn't get to see him that often. So, while he tried to be in my life, he wasn't able to. As a result, I found myself getting angry that he wasn't around and trying to prove that I was worth loving by being 'a good kid'. And I excelled at looking the part.

Fast-forward many years and I have a life that is marked by frustration and bitterness for not having the parents I wanted and always trying to prove to others that I am worth loving. Whether it was through how I excelled in school, work, athletics, or just making people laugh so they will like me, I craved approval so I could sense that I was worthy. What I found was that when people approved of me, I was happy, but their approval didn't always last. When people would reject me, leave, or even if I offended them, I would be devastated. I mean crushed. I was worthless. So I would re-double my efforts to prove myself worthy again. But the stress of trying to be perfect was an overwhelming burden. I was hiding the hurt so people would like me. I got so good at hiding, I had even convinced myself!

But here's what I've discovered. In Jesus, we are fully and perfectly loved and approved of by God. The One who created us loves us. He became flesh and dwelt among us, and in the Person of Jesus, declared to me and you that we can lay down our need to prove ourselves; Jesus has done it for us. Jesus proved none of us are sufficient and all are in need of rescue. And then, He rescued us! All we need to do is believe. For me, the result has been a complete freeing of the weight of needing to prove myself. Realizing that I am already perfectly loved removes the burden I place on other broken humans of needing to love me perfectly so I can feel good about myself. Do you see the freedom in this?

Roger, like many others, came to trust in the life, death, and resurrection of Jesus for his own. It didn't happen from one conversation, but over time, his eyes were opened to the beauty of Jesus and the freedom found in Him. When we listen and share our story in light of where they are, we are given many opportunities to tell of who Jesus is and what He has done in incredibly compelling ways.

INVITING

When someone hears the good news of Jesus and how He has tangibly worked in your life, they often wonder what their next step is. Instead of shying away from it, help them process what they are thinking and feeling, as well as what it means for them. For some, the next step will be inviting them to trust in Jesus and what He has declared in light of where they are. For others, taking a look at the Scriptures with you is their next step. The list goes on, as this is determined on a case-by-case basis, so dependence on the Spirit's leading will be a must.

Before you decide what to invite someone into, it's important to consider a couple of things.

First, have you listened to what your friend needs or is actually looking for? Have they made any indication as to what they think they need to do in light of what you have been discussing with them? Often times you'll get hints as to where they are and what would be a good next step from their perspective versus what you think is the best move.

Second, are you listening to the Spirit of God and His leading? Have you considered asking "What's next, Lord?" in regard to the person you are discipling? The goal is inviting them to take a step of faith in what Jesus is revealing and where He is leading. Praying something like "what's next?" is a helpful way to wait and listen for the Spirit's leading. Remember, He loves your friend and desires to see them trust and follow Jesus even more than you do! Seek His leading.

TEACHING

In Matthew 28:20 Jesus finishes out the commission to, *"Go therefore and make disciples,"* with the words, *"teach them to observe all I commanded."* The aim of our *"teaching"* Jesus says isn't the transfer of information, but instead walking in joyful allegiance to the One who's perfect obedience has been attributed to us (Rom. 4). In other words, to *"observe* (obey) *all He's commanded,"* in light of the gospel, is an issue of the heart... not of the will. If it was an issue of the will, Paul wouldn't say, *"I do not nullify the grace of God, for if righteousness were through the law, then Christ died for no purpose."* (Galatians 2:21)

With this understanding in mind, discipling others *"to observe all Jesus commanded"* is seen as a process of teaching others to WAIT on the Spirit as they seek Jesus, WATCH for where He is at work, and

WALK in the fruit that the Spirit bears in their midst.

Now, that statement may have caused you to do a double take. I know I (Russ) did when I first saw this. I was a pastor/planter who was well versed in Scripture and ready to remind people at a moment's notice of this truth: "Not only did Jesus command us to *'teach them to obey all I commanded,'* He also said, *'Whoever has my commandments and keeps them, he it is who loves me.'*" (John 14:21)

Two statements. Both good and true. But when interpreted and used as if they exist on a separate island by themselves, independent of everything else Jesus has declared, they become dangerous. We wind up using a promise that Jesus made: "There will be the fruit of obedience in the lives of those who love me," as marching orders: "You need to prove your love by obeying me."

How did we get here when Jesus plainly says in the very next chapter, "*I am the vine; you are the branches. Whoever abides in me and I in him, he it is that bears much fruit, for apart from me you can do nothing*"? (John 15:5) Does "nothing" not mean nothing, as in zilch, zero, nada?

How did we get to a place of working to fix our lives and the lives of those around us when Jesus Himself, in that same chapter, says His *"Father is the vinedresser,"* as in the gardener who owns and oversees every aspect of the vineyard? (John 15:1) Have you ever seen a branch take on the role of a gardener?

The Apostle Paul, when addressing the Galatians who were pushing works of fleshly obedience to obtain and maintain the righteousness we need, said, *"in Christ Jesus neither circumcision nor uncircumcision counts for anything, but only faith working through love."* (Gal 5:6) Paul knew the teachings of Jesus, and he knew your fleshly obedience, on your best day, is of no value because fleshly righteousness is a worthless counterfeit. But the righteousness of God, born in us by the Spirit of Christ, is perfect! Perfect because it is not ours, nor of us. God fulfills His commands by way of His Son, in us. For, *"he who began a good work in you will bring it to completion."* (Philippians 1:6) This is a promise, and it has nothing to do with your ability to see this fruit, nor your ability to taste it. For as 2 Corinthians 4:18 states, our faith is *"not on what is seen"* (our progress), *"but on what is unseen"* (the Person of Jesus). (NIV)

So, what does this look like? While there are many different ways "joyful allegiance" may be worked out in you and those you disciple, here's an example to consider.

When Paul and I (Gino) met, he desired to honor and glorify God with his whole life. Whether it was as a husband and father, or in the demands of his busy workplace, he truly wanted to walk in obedience to God and bring Him glory. I recall him telling me early in our relationship, "I read the Scriptures and Jesus clearly says, 'Love God and love your neighbor,' and then I look around and ask myself, 'Do I really love my neighbor? How do I love my neighbor?'"

For Paul, most of the answers to his "How do I love my neighbor?" question, revolved around digging deeper into the truth of the Bible and/or listening to more sermons and teachings so that he would go and share his faith with his neighbors. While this is valuable, Paul didn't need convincing. He was already convinced; actually, it was stronger than that, he was convicted. To Paul, to say he loved God and loved others without pointing to people he was tangibly loving, seemed as if he really didn't believe Jesus' commands.

So we, along with our wives, children, and a couple other families, prayerfully took steps toward loving others in our lives. How did we do this? We followed the Spirit's leading and looked for opportunities to develop relationships with people, to be present in their lives and listen to their stories. We'd throw parties to gather people together and we naturally started meeting each others' needs in any way we could (watching kids, bringing meals, sharing rides, going to ballgames to support, etc.).

As the relationship with our new friends developed, Paul learned he had a natural gift for sharing his story and need for Jesus in light of our friends' stories. In time, some of our new friends began to trust in Jesus and Paul learned to invite them to follow Jesus with us, teaching them to do the same with others.

Paul was taught how to trust the Spirit's leading in his life and begin to intentionally and tangibly love others around him. As a result, he not only experienced obedience as joyful allegiance to Jesus, he has repeated this process with a number of people and is now leading a new church family.

When it comes to teaching others, may we be even more convinced by what God has declared in the Scriptures about those we are teaching than what we can temporarily see.

May we be mindful that discipling others goes beyond teaching them to know what Jesus said. In a time of information overload, it's easy to think the need is more sermons, more podcasts, more Bible studies rather than teaching others to walk in joyful allegiance to Jesus, trusting Him to bear fruit when and how He chooses.

6

NOW, FAIL FORWARD

*GRACE FOR THOSE
ON THE GO*

Hopefully you have gained some insight throughout this book around the immense connection between slowing down and the extension of the message and medium of Jesus to the world. And hopefully you have gained some practical insights around how the mission to disciple lies at the heart of this connection.

But.... before you run forward, there is one last thing we want to be sure to leave with you. It's a lesson we have learned, relearned, and need to continue to learn as practitioners. We call it, "grace for those on the go," and the name fits because it is our frailty, foolishness, and failures that will be front and center when we slow down to love and disciple others where they are.

What are some of the ways this frailty and foolishness shows itself? Apathy, fear, desire for human approval, and love of self (just to name a few). These will become more evident than ever, causing us to do and say some really dumb things around people we're getting to know. Instead of getting into all of the specifics around these struggles, let's just generalize our shortcomings into two categories: bailing and blending. In John 17, Jesus prayed, in essence, that we would "*be in the world*," but "*not of the world*." Bailing is when we retreat from the mission and fail to involve ourselves as true members of our cities and our world. Blending is when we resemble those we're called to carry good news to in such a way you'd never know this message of freedom has set us free. At some point, we will all bail from some opportunities God clearly has invited us into. Typically, it's a missed invitation here or being silent when we were called to speak. Our frailty and foolishness show up as bailing.

Anyone who has taken the Great Commission seriously knows what we're talking about. And if you haven't experienced this yet, it's coming. Which is why we thought it would be good to share something we cling to often, especially in times of seeming failure. The lesson is found in a familiar scene in John's gospel.

He came to Simon Peter, who said to Him, "*Lord, do you wash my feet?*" Jesus answered him, "*What I am doing you do not understand now, but afterward you will understand.*" Peter said to Him, "*You shall never wash my feet.*" Jesus answered him, "*If I do not wash you, you have no share with me.*" Simon Peter said to Him, "*Lord, not my feet only but also my hands and my head!*" Jesus said to him, "*The one who has bathed does not need to wash, except for his feet, but is completely clean. And you are clean, but not every one of you.*" (John 13:6-10)

In John 13, Jesus is in a private upper room with all twelve of His disciples sharing a Passover meal. The disciples don't know it, but Jesus is just hours away from being arrested, on trial, flogging, and death. At least for now, all seems normal for these Jewish guys around a table for the Passover celebration.

Jesus, keenly aware of what's about to transpire, knows these are the last moments He'll spend with these guys before the very purpose of His coming, namely His death, plays out.

As a way to drive home the weight of how Jesus is about to sacrificially serve a hell-bent world in His dying, He takes on the role reserved for the lowest of servants in the middle of the meal and begins to wash the feet of everyone present.

I'm sure what Jesus was doing made everyone uncomfortable, but only Peter had the courage to verbalize what everyone was thinking, *"Lord, do you wash my feet?"* Who doesn't love Peter? He's kind of like Uncle Paulie from the Rocky film series. He speaks loudly, unwisely, out of turn, and often ignorantly. He's the one that adds a bit of comedy in a weighty moment.

Jesus tells Peter there's a larger reality beyond His serving them right now (alluding to the cross), one that Peter didn't get at the moment. Then Jesus reminds Peter, *"If I do not wash you, you have no share with me."* Peter concedes, but then responds like an overly emotional Junior High School student would (or Uncle Paulie). Essentially, Peter says, "Fine. I'm so unworthy to be served by you; wash everything then!"

Jesus—ever so patiently—responds this way,

"The one who has bathed does not need to wash, except for his feet, but is completely clean. And you are clean, but not every one of you." (John 13:10)

Jesus tells Peter that he's already clean (with an obvious reference to Judas the betrayer, the unclean one). We take Jesus' declaration to Peter and the other ten disciples being "completely clean" as a reference to the spiritual cleanness, forgiveness and perfection that Peter already possesses due to the work that Jesus is just a few days away from accomplishing. In Jesus, we were crucified (Gal 2:20), we are perfectly righteous (2 Cor. 5:21), we are completely sanctified (Heb. 10:14), and we are washed and clean (1 Cor. 6:11). In Christ, we are the ones who have bathed! We have no need to wash ourselves again because we are completely immersed in Christ. Amen!

But, check this out. Jesus follows this up with another comforting truth. He says those who are bathed don't need to wash, except for their feet. Jesus alludes to the fact here that even though we are perfect in Him, as we go about our lives as the deeply flawed people we are, our feet are going to get dirty. There will inevitably be times we live and act in the flesh (the independent self) instead of walk by the Spirit.

Even the way Jesus says this seems sympathetic toward us. Failure and selfishness are inevitable. You are as sure to sin as you go about on His mission as your feet are to get dirty as you walk outside (especially with first century foot gear). This does not surprise Jesus. He's the one who told us it would happen.

Your feet are going to get dirty, but remember, you are completely clean. You are perfect in Him. Such good news!

Now consider this: there is an obvious connection between the mission of God to carry the Good News to our neighbors and feet in the New Testament:

> *And how are they to preach unless they are sent? As it is written, "How beautiful are the feet of those who preach the good news!" (Romans 10:15)*

Could it be, along with generally referring to our daily need for grace and forgiveness as righteous wrecks, Jesus alludes here to the Great Commission? Of course! The entirety of the Christian life and the life of the Church is framed within the call to make disciples as we go, by foot, to the places where we live, work, and play as His ambassadors. And for this mission we will need to daily cling to His grace in the face of our bailing and blending.

Consider what Jesus is telling Peter here in light of the challenging task of living among our neighbors as missionaries:

- You're clean. Perfect in Jesus, who is your life, because of what He's done and declared you.

- You're going to fail. Failure in life (specifically in mission) is as inevitable as getting your feet dirty as you walk around outside.

- You're in need of ongoing cleansing (forgiveness) for your dirty feet (deeds of the flesh).

- Remember and cling to #1.

The good news is, in Jesus, we have the promise from God that He *"will remember their sins no more."* (Hebrews 8:12) He always stands ready and delighted to continually wash our feet that are dirty with frailty, foolishness, and other fleshy displays. We have forever forgiveness in Jesus while seeking to be on His mission of loving our neighbors and sharing the good news shaping our souls.

Often times the tension, awkwardness, challenge, and straight up failure as disciple-makers is enough to cause people to run back into their Christian safe havens, never to return again. Our missional guilt paralyzes us. The gospel is the exact power we need to take a deep breath, know that we're loved, forgiven, and clean, and to get back on our feet and onto the missional journey God has invited us to join Him in.

The litmus test is whom you're resting in as you journey on.

Nothing less.

Nothing more.

So now we invite you to get your feet dirty.

CONCLUSION

Like a carpenter who takes raw materials and turns them into beautiful works of art, Jesus is the One who makes all things new. As a network, we have found rest in this life-changing news. And as a network, we have found rest in knowing we do nothing more than carry the raw materials of love and discipleship into our unique context. As leaders focus on equipping disciples in these timeless functions, new families form around good food, Good News and good conversation.

These families, living and declaring the message of freedom, are an expression of the scattered and gathered Church in their context. In its most simplistic form, whether through micro-churches that gather in homes, pubs, cross-fit gyms, or on beaches, and also through larger conventional churches made up of missional communities, this is how we believe our vision— **"to see everyone experience the freedom and family found at the table Jesus has prepared"**— becomes a reality.

If you are longing to see others experience the freedom and family found in Jesus, we'd love to discuss how we could join you in that endeavor.

Give us a shout.

hello@thetablenetwork.com
www.thetablenetwork.com

APPENDICES

WHO SLOWS DOWN
WITH VICKY?

*HOW WE'RE HELPING OTHERS
MAKE DISCIPLES*

Do you remember earlier when we told you about Bob? Bob has friends who he loves deeply and longs to see come to follow Jesus. Yet most of Bob's friends have absolutely zero interest in ever attending any event or gathering at his church. Sadly, Bob has missed this fact. He gives a lot of his time, money, and other resources to try to make his church and her events top notch and attractive for his friends, but it matters very little. For the most part, Bob's friends aren't looking for a church to attend.

Do you see the disconnect here? No matter how amazing Bob's church is, a good percentage of his friends aren't coming because they aren't looking for a church service.

If you asked one of Bob's friends, Vicky, what she thinks about Christianity and the church, she would tell you (we know because one of our leaders met Vicky in line at a coffee shop and she told him this!). From Vicky's personal experience, she believes the church offers nothing but long-winded calls to a life no one can live and a community of self-righteous people who think they can. With that perspective, no matter how she arrived there, it makes sense why she isn't taking advantage of Bob's invitations to "go to church" with him.

As you listen to Vicky's story, you may realize she's one of over 200 million people in America (upwards of 70% of the population) who have no interest in attending a church service or gathering of any kind (see "The Permanent Revolution" by Hirsch & Catchim).

To be clear, we are not saying there is no value in the approach Bob has been a part of. Based on the numbers we just gave you, 30% of the population would be interested in coming to a church gathering or event. And those people matter greatly. We are glad for the faithful witness of many saints (some who are leading in our network) through these methods. And still, we can't look past the 70% either.

At the core of the Table Network is the desire to see everyone experience the freedom and family found at the table Jesus has prepared. When we say "everyone", we truly mean, "everyone." We are seeing that reaching the 70% of the population requires not a better approach, but rather a different approach than what will reach the 30%.

It requires an approach that recognizes every disciple has the Holy Spirit and a table to gather others around good food, Good News and good conversation.

What does this approach actually look like in our day and time?

Let's consider the issue. If Vicky (and millions like her) won't come to anything the church offers in order to learn about the Person and work of Jesus, we have to ask ourselves some questions:

- Who slows down to meet Vicky where she is and takes the time necessary to disciple her in the freedom found in Jesus alone?

- Who equips, shepherds, and frees up the disciples who will disciple Vicky?

- What does an expression of the church look like that provides Vicky and her friends with a family to belong to on their way to belief and involvement in the things of Jesus?

Questions like these help us move our vision from a statement we hold true to a life we are living. As a network comprised of ministry experience that spans an array of contexts, we believe the pursuit of this vision is marked by empowering the timeless things we see in the life of Jesus, Paul, and the New Testament church:

MISSION - The timeless functions of discipleship in the hands of every believer.

MESSAGE - The scandalous grace of God at the heart of everything we're saying.

MEDIUM - The formation of simple church families unique to each context.

MOBILIZERS - The role of every leader to model and empower these endeavors.

Not only do we want Bob to know the foundational truths defining the mission, message, and medium of Jesus, we also want him to be equipped in the timeless functions that bring them to the world.

We want him to know he is free to think less about discipleship and a new church forming through the lens of a rented auditorium, and more about how to be a good dinner host. We want him to know he can trade tools like ProPresenter for a trip to Sur La Table and exchange a well-crafted sermon for a weekly discussion around good food and good wine.

Bob is free to return to this ancient, minimalist approach to see his life, his family's life, and the lives of his friends experience the freedom and family found in Jesus. All he needs to get started is the Spirit of God, a willingness to learn, and a table (which can be borrowed from any local coffee shop or pub if needed).

With a heart to empower Bob, as well as any church planter or pastor, we often hear, "I love the Biblical foundation and the simplicity in your approach. But how are you guys actually empowering these things? Tell me exactly what you do to see this happen."

The answer to this question is laid out in three phases:

Phase 1 // Information // RESOURCES & LABS

We live in a day where skepticism and cynicism serve as the framing narrative for much of society. As a result, everyday disciples like Bob, church planters, and church leaders are often left wondering how to meet people where they are. With the desire to come alongside them, we have created a number of resources such as books, blogs, and a weekly podcast. In addition to this we are hosting Labs for those who are open to taking a look at how the beliefs and behaviors of old are shaping gospel movements today. No programs to implement. No forms of ministry to adopt. We just look at the timeless functions of the church, discipleship, and leadership for any and every context.

Phase 2 // Imitation // COHORTS

As stated earlier in this book, Jesus used a Hebraic approach when developing leaders. Rather than help them think their way into a new way of acting (the Hellenistic approach), He invited the disciples to come act their way into a new way of thinking. In keeping with His approach, our Cohorts are a one-year journey for those who are hungry to learn, love, and make disciples. The journey champions the limited margin participants have, while simultaneously providing them with content, coaching, and a community to learn and implement with.

CONTENT: With the vision before us for everyone, the need before us is not thousands of new church expressions, but millions. This means we need an approach that goes beyond the normal approach focused on just empowering leaders. As in, we need an approach that works from the harvest back, not vice versa. By starting there, we found the truths at the heart of the message, medium, and mission of Jesus are not only conducive to seeing believers live in them, they're also directly in line with the misconceptions keeping many of those outside the faith at arm's length. Unearthing these truths, and placing them in the hands of each and every believer in a way they in turn can do the same with those they're discipling, is what we created our Reclaim resource to accomplish.

In addition to this, we provide leaders with other resources known as Ministry Primers that intentionally don't tell leaders what to do, but instead help them look to the Scriptures and hear from the Spirit as they: 1) develop their unique gifts/voice as a leader; 2) craft their story in a way that speaks to those around them; 3) apprentice leaders in, rather than for, the work of the ministry; 4) create a scattered and gathered church rhythm that empowers the furtherance of the mission; and 5) develop a leadership and financial structure that champion's movement for any and every context.

COACHING: As practitioners who personally know the trials and tribulations a leader faces as they set out to disciple others and see new expressions form and existing ones flourish, we place a high priority on coaching. Which is why every Cohort comes not only with the content resources needed, but a coach who is committed to walking alongside a leader as they implement things for their context.

COMMUNITY: Content is key, and a coach is a real need... but having a family of like-minded leaders to learn, laugh, share, and serve with as you journey forward is a must. The authentic community we crave is birthed out of the pursuit of a common mission. By God's grace, we are seeing Cohorts provide both as leaders come together on a regular basis throughout the journey.

Phase 3 // Innovation // COLLECTIVES

Once leaders have journeyed through a Learning Cohort and disciple-making movement is underway, our focus is simply connecting the leaders who've emerged with others in the Table family into networks we refer to as Collectives. These regional networks provide leaders with a means of ongoing coaching and care, further development in their unique ministry wiring, a community of leaders to work with, and a way to leverage some of their resources for the multiplication of disciples and church families throughout their region.

Walking with others through these phases of information, imitation, and innovation are how we are empowering a growing number of people to extend the freedom and family of Jesus to all. We believe Jesus has called everyone to this mission, and we believe everyone should be equipped for the journey.

So, whether you are an everyday disciple or a church planter or pastor who wants to see the gospel spread to everyone in your context, we would love to join you.

WHAT ABOUT BOB'S PASTOR?

*HOW LEADERS CAN EMPOWER
EVERY MEMBER FOR MISSION*

Remember at the beginning of this book, when we introduced you to Bob? Well, Bob's church has a pastor. And contrary to popular belief, the two don't need to be at odds when it comes to the ministry needs and different ministry styles needed to love their city. In fact, from what we have experienced, both of them can be instrumental in working together to see a disciple-making movement occur. Here's how.

Bob's pastor is like a lot of other faithful

pastors. For starters, he genuinely loves Jesus and above everything else wants the people in his life (including his family) to know, trust, and love Jesus, too. In addition, Bob's pastor loves the church. His home is regularly open to them, he frequently flexes his schedule to meet people when it works for them, and his mind and heart are often occupied with the burdens of those experiencing trials and the joys of those experiencing triumphs.

Bob's pastor feels ultimately responsible for the health and growth of the church and his staff. On top of all this, let's not forget, Sunday is coming... something which is always looming in his mind.

Despite the burdens, expectations, and demands on his time, he still considers his job to be a privilege and a joy. He wouldn't have it any other way.

Bob's pastor also has a genuine burden for his community and broader region to know and worship Jesus. He most likely cares about this more than anyone in his church and yet always seems to be spinning his wheels when it comes to reaching those outside the faith. In fact, he's frustrated. Maybe even feeling a bit defeated.

If there's a book, he's read it. If there's a

conference, he's attended it. He always has a missional application in his sermons, and has explicitly preached on the Great Commission... passionately. He's even tried implementing a few things at his church to help jump start missional living among the members. From missional training classes to practically serving their city on a weekend to mobilizing their small groups to throw block parties, there's been a myriad of efforts.

But nothing seems to truly materialize into a way of life for the people in his care.

If this is you, we want you to know we understand. We've been there. Not only do we love serving the Bobs of this world as they seek to connect with the Vickys, we love to come alongside Bob's pastor as he seeks to equip and empower the disciple-making culture he longs to see in their local church family. And to do so in such a way where Bob's pastor doesn't feel like he needs to quit his job or blow everything up in order to see these things happen.

With that said, here are some tensions pastors live with and the shifts we have found necessary to begin seeing a disciple-making movement take flight in their local churches.

Living as Missionaries

Pastors personally know the tension between preaching good news from a pulpit and preaching good news as a missionary in their neighborhoods. There are a lot of pastors who are very skilled in applying the gospel to their people in a variety of different topics, trials, and texts. But can they remember the last time they shared the Good News with one of their neighbors?

Oddly enough, this lack of missional practice and experience doesn't keep pastors from telling their people they ought to be on mission. I (Tony) can pull up sermons from years past where I boldly called people to mission, with Scriptures in hand, all the while I personally didn't have one single sustained discipling relationship with anyone outside the faith.

While there are a number of negative side effects with this inconsistency, two things always happen when pastors preach a theology of mission from their platform without the reality of mission in their lives. At best they simply transfer their missional theory to their people so they, too, can be versed in the missional applications of the incarnation without actually being present with people, learning to share the gospel in light of where their neighbors are. At worst their missional admonitions hit their people like an unattainable law as it comes across very idealistic and lofty, void of the experiences and stories to help ground the Great Commission in the reality of normal people living everyday lives.

Late professor and Bible teacher, Howard Hendricks, once said, "You can teach what you know, but only reproduce who you are." While this statement applies to all areas of life, I believe it is especially relevant to living as a missionary. You can teach about mission until you're blue in the face, but do not expect your people to live missionally if you are not doing so yourself.

At this point some of you may be thinking how you can work your way out of your bubble in order to begin being on mission. If that's you, I want to share a brief story from my life.

In 2014, I came to the realization that I had not discipled anyone outside the faith in a very long time. This was despite being known as the "missional guy" on a large church staff of almost 20 pastors and directors. Perhaps this was because we had a couple annual outreach events on our campus calendar and I was always talking about mission. I knew

Jesus was calling me back on His mission as a practitioner of all I had been telling everyone else they ought to be doing, but I didn't know where to start.

One day I had the idea to join in with a family that was attending the campus I was pastoring at the time. They never really got involved beyond attending Sunday services, but that was why I was drawn to them.

This couple spent most of their spare time with their tribe in the places they were and knew how to throw house parties and practice hospitality. They had a ton of friends who were outside the faith and outside of faith communities. They were wondering how to better disciple their friends and I was looking for friends. I simply asked them if I could join in.

I started attending parties (like Jesus did) and slowly began making friends. Some of these friendships turned into discipleship relationships and, over time, we eventually saw a couple of our friends get baptized, join church families, and now they're growing as disciple-makers in the places they live and work.

Even though I eventually left the church I was pastoring at that time to pursue living as a missionary and seeing churches form from the harvest, this season helped me rediscover the mission as a practitioner, not just a preacher of missional theology or theory.

I share this brief story to encourage you. You can do this. You can make the mission a priority. It may not play out exactly like my story, but who cares? Instead of being the one in the pulpit telling your folks in the pew to be on mission, you'll be joining them in the pubs as an actual missionary. Trust me, modeling the mission will speak much louder than the preset volume your sound guy has on your sweet face microphone.

In addition, being a missional practitioner will also help you to be an equipper with loads of stories to help stir your people toward practical discipleship among their neighbors. Stories help stoke the missional imagination of those you're equipping as they, too, can picture themselves throwing simple house parties for the folks they are meeting around town. As they hear about how you connected the gospel to a basic struggle or interest your neighbor shared around a campfire last weekend, they too, can imagine carrying good news to their friends.

As you can see, being a missionary will be necessary if you desire to be an equipper, so let's take a look at the necessity of this New Testament leadership function for the making of disciples who make disciples.

Leading as Equippers

Pastors find most of their time and energy is devoted to managing and overseeing week-to-week ministries and the staff and volunteers who lead them. In addition to this, they also feel the need to keep up with the growing shepherding needs of their people. With this in mind, it's hard for pastors to imagine how they can carve out time to begin the long journey of equipping their people to make disciples. Especially since so many of them have tried, from time to time, various things they thought were going to spark movement. As mentioned before, we know the tension and frustration here and yet, there's this nagging reality in the Scriptures about the nature of their roles they feel they can no longer ignore.

The primary function of any leader, including the pastor-teacher types, is, *"to equip the saints for the work of the ministry."* (Eph 4:11-12) Based on New Testament teachings, we know *"the work of the ministry"* refers to something much richer than handing out bulletins and finding empty seats for the folks arriving late to a Sunday service. (Pssst!

It refers to the Great Commission and how each member of the church is uniquely gifted for the making of disciples.)

As pastors, we know you feel the weight to equip, we also know you are under some pressure to assimilate people. To move folks from being attenders, to becoming members, into small groups, to becoming givers and ultimately into servants. While we all know in our heart of hearts it's not about the numbers, we sure talk a lot about them at elder & staff meetings. It's hard to escape this feeling when it seems to be the chief metric for health in the vast majority of churches.

While there may be a much deeper shift needed to take place in regard to what you value, resource, and celebrate as a church family, we have found the change really does need to start with you.

We need to place a higher value on equipping disciples to make disciples and less of a value on the conveyer belt of assimilation.

When we do this, we make disciples of Jesus who follow Him into their everyday spaces as missionaries, instead of making disciples of our churches who find their spare time dominated with church activity week after week as they drive right past their neighbors on the way to church yet again.

You don't have to be the sole equipper in your church. In fact, you don't even need to be the best equipper, but you do need to devote some time to it if you long for those following your lead to begin seeing themselves as disciples who make disciples where they live, work, and play.

In addition to being missionaries and equippers there are two more vital axioms we have found that pastors/elders everywhere will need to embrace if the longing is to see a disciple-making movement.

Freeing People Up

I learned the hard truth that a church is what it does. What I mean is this, churches can explicitly say from their stages, social media, and mission statements that they value the making of disciples and the spread of the gospel in their city, and at the same time, implicitly communicate something different by what they celebrate, announce, promote, and place on the calendar.

A pastor can preach his guts out about every disciple spending time with their neighbors, but as soon as they get out of the auditorium they're handed a card highlighting two events in the coming month just after they were passionately pressured to stop by the booths highlighting ministry volunteer opportunities. The culture of a church will always implicitly communicate the true values of a church. What you're explicitly calling people to in your sermon series will eventually be drowned out.

While you might not be to the place where you can begin deprogramming your entire church in order to free up everyone's time to walk in the things you call them to, you can, however, free up certain people to step away from the busyness of church activity so they can be equipped for the slow journey of making disciples among those outside the faith.

One thought that may help: the people who are probably best suited for this are among the 80% of people who are not at church every time the doors are open. I've found those folks really love Jesus and they have a heart for their neighbors...who they actually know and hang with because they didn't sign up for everything and anything. This shift in thinking frees you up to have a positive and hopeful perspective of an otherwise demonized group in your church. With a new posture toward the "disconnected" you can shift your efforts from connecting them inward to mobilizing them outward. Champion this.

Being Okay With Spontaneous Expansion

This is generally the hardest shift for us as leaders. Why? Because many of us have been handed a "biblical" view of church leadership and authority that will fight us on this one the whole way.

What happens when you equip some people in your church to go make disciples among those uninterested in the church in hopes they see new church communities form and it actually happens (like Jesus promised)?

I'm sure you'll celebrate the fruit of the gospel among these folks, but will you then try to assimilate them? Will you pressure the leader you just equipped to plant the gospel among the unchurched to get these new folks to the membership class? Are you okay with them getting baptized in a pool on a Saturday instead of in a service on Sunday? What if they are never comfortable coming to YOUR Sunday gathering, but rather refer to the small little gathering led by the leaders you equipped as THEIR CHURCH? Are you ready to see new church families form?

How does all this sit with you? You're

probably a combination of completely nervous about the notion and at the same time totally wishing it would happen. If, on the other hand, you went to your library to grab your book on biblical eldership just know it was completely normal for new churches to spontaneously spring up as the gospel was planted in Acts. When we follow the timeline, it wasn't until 1-2 years later that Paul sent other leaders back to these churches not to train, but to "appoint elders" (Acts 14; Titus 1).

We don't need to have it all figured out. The best thing we can remind ourselves of is how this is Jesus' mission and Jesus' church. He is the one building His church, not us. We've spent countless hours and dollars on training and sending methods thinking that it's these things that are getting the job done. Have you ever thought Jesus is building His church in spite of these things instead of because of them? As I look at the book of Acts, I see a group of apostles more so wrapped-up and responding to a work of Jesus – and less so rolling out a 10-year plan with a detailed execution strategy.

There's something so life-giving about letting go of this thing called control, that was an illusion in the first place, and asking Jesus to help us faithfully respond to a work that is

His and His alone.

> *"Spontaneous expansion must be free: it cannot be under our control; and consequently it is utterly vain to say, as I constantly hear men say, that we desire to see spontaneous expansion, and yet must maintain our control. If we want to see spontaneous expansion we must establish native Churches free from our control."* *(Roland Allen, The Spontaneous Expansion of the Church: And the Causes That Hinder It)*

To Kick Things Off... Start Slow and Small

As a network, we've been sharing a lot of what we've written here for a while now and have witnessed a number of reactions in pastor/leaders. We've seen the look on a pastor's face when missional despair sets in. The moment they realize their church has tried various approaches, is tired, and still lacks a disciple-making culture.

We've been face to face with pastors who wanted to change their Sunday sermon on a Saturday at 5pm after sitting in a 1Day workshop about disciple-making, thinking somehow preaching their scribbled notes will be the magic bullet.

Somewhere between giving up completely and fixing your church in a single Sunday is the leader who knows this is going to take some time and patience. And so, I have two words for any of you who are being stirred to start prioritizing the mission as a missionary and an equipper: baby steps. I mean, come on, we couldn't write a book with a chapter called "What About Bob?" and not talk about baby steps.

We often say,

"Think small if you want to go far. Move slow if you want to go fast."

"Think small" because it is disciples who make disciples. The gospel spreads and discipleship happens through them, and this, in relationships where people are personally known. The more disciples made, the farther you go. So, if you truly "want to go fast," follow Jesus' example and "move slow." Making disciples among your neighbors who aren't interested in the church is a slow and challenging process, and so is seeing some disciple-making movement take root and grow in a local church. But it is needed; and it can happen. We've seen it. And we're here to serve if you're looking for some fellow practitioners to journey with.

ABOUT THE AUTHORS

Russ Johnson is the founder of The Table Network and is responsible for setting direction and empowering partnership development efforts. Originally from the Tampa Bay area, Russ spent 15 years prior to TTN planting and pastoring new and existing churches in North Carolina and Chicago. He lives in Fort Myers, FL now with his wife, Christa, and their three children, where he is making disciples and training leaders.

Gino Curcuruto came to The Table Network as an experienced leadership coach and is responsible for organizing direction and empowering coaching efforts. Originally from L.A., Gino now resides in Philadelphia with his wife, Jill, and their 4 kids, where he leads a business and is planting The Table Philadelphia. Link up with him on Twitter: @ginoc

Tony Sorci had ten years experience pastoring in traditional church contexts before coming to The Table Network in 2014. He is now responsible for guiding direction and empowering training efforts. In addition to his role with the network, Tony leads a church family known as Communitas in the Chicagoland area where he lives with his wife Pam and their four kids.

LEARNING LABS

Skepticism and cynicism serve as the prevailing narrative for most in our society. In light of this, most disciples are left wondering how to build relationships with their neighbors, meet them where they are with good news, and form communities fitting for them.

Our Learning Labs are designed for everyday people to envision simple ways in which they can begin living out this mission.

■ ■ ■ ■ ■ ■ ■ ■ ■ ■ ■ ■

- TAUGHT BY PROVEN PRACTITIONERS FOR EVERYDAY PEOPLE WHO ARE HUNGRY TO REACH THEIR NEIGHBORS.

- COVERING A VARIETY OF TOPICS RELATED TO THE MISSION OF EXTENDING THE FREEDOM AND FAMILY OF JESUS IN YOUR CONTEXT.

- FORMATS ARE BOTH ONLINE AND IN PERSON THROUGHOUT CITIES BOTH LARGE AND SMALL.

- RANGE FROM LUNCH HOUR CONVERSATIONS TO ALL DAY EVENTS, AND CAN BE HOSTED BY ANYONE LOOKING TO PARTNER WITH US.

For more info visit us at thetablenetwork.com

LEARNING COHORTS

Rather than helping his disciples think their way into a new way of acting (the Hellenistic approach), Jesus invited them to into a new way of thinking by way of participation (the Hebraic approach). In keeping with this approach toward equipping, our Learning Cohorts work as "on the job training" while leveraging content, coaching, and the role of community to help leaders find rest, slow down, and extend freedom and family to others. New church families gathering around good food, Good News and good conversation is the natural result.

■ ■ ■ ■ ■ ■ ■ ■ ■ ■ ■ ■ ■

- LED BY SEASONED PRACTITIONERS USING ONLINE COMMUNITY DISCUSSIONS

- 24, ONE HOUR SESSIONS WITH OTHERS HUNGRY TO MAKE DISCIPLES.

- STAY IN YOUR UNIQUE CONTEXT AS YOU LEARN AND IMPLEMENT.

- GAIN ACCESS TO ALL OF OUR TRAINING TOOLS AT NO ADDITIONAL COST.

- ONLY PAY $100 A MONTH THROUGH A PAY-IT-FORWARD MODEL.

THE SLOW DOWN is a podcast hosted by everyday people who are navigating life and discipleship by the seat of their pants and the grace of God. We take an unfiltered look at how the finished work of Jesus has set us free from the exhausting madness of trying to fix our lives and the lives of others. Listen in on our ongoing dialogue concerning the simple, but rather hard realities that accompany the practice of extending the freedom and family of Jesus to those we encounter.

This is our open confessional of how we've fallen short, and our stories of what God has taught us along the way. The mission Jesus has invited us into needs honest, helpful, and hopeful dialogue - and we intend to give it our best shot with this podcast.

AVAILABLE NOW ON iTUNES, GOOGLE MUSIC, STITCHER, PODBEAN, AND MORE.

For more info visit us at thetablenetwork.com